A BOOK OF PRAYERS

For the journey of faith

This edition copyright © 1995 Lion Publishing

Published by
Lion Publishing plc
Sandy Lane West, Oxford, England
ISBN 0 7459 3358 0

Albatross Books Pty Ltd
PO Box 320, Sutherland, NSW 2232, Australia
ISBN 0 7324 1320 6

First edition 1995
10 9 8 7 6 5 4 3 2 1 0

A catalogue record for this book is available
from the British Library

Printed and bound in Singapore

A BOOK OF PRAYERS
for
The Journey of Faith

LION
Giftlines

Contents

Introduction

For some people, prayer seems to be the easiest thing in the world. Their prayer is thoughtful and fluent – and it seems they can turn it on and off like a tap!

But for most of us prayer is often quite hard and sometimes impossible. We can't help wondering whether God is really interested in the everyday things of our lives.

All of us who pray have times when we feel distant from God. There are occasions – perhaps even long periods of time – when we seem to be waiting for God. All we can say of him is that he doesn't seem to be around.

But as we continue to be available to him, we become aware that he is in fact all around us –

and within us. He is everywhere and very close. As we open our hearts to God, he'll make himself known to us in his own way and in his own time. The particular way he deals with each of us can never be predicted, demanded or explained. It will be unique.

The unique nature of our relationship with God means that personal, spontaneous prayer is important. We 'talk' to God in prayer. But this is not always easy, especially if we are new to prayer. This is where written prayers can help. We have much in common as human beings, so other people's prayers can reflect the desires and fears of our own heart.

This anthology has been compiled for those who are on a journey of faith — with all its joy and challenges, difficulties and doubts. We hope it will give you help and encouragement for the next steps of the journey.

'God loves us. His motive in making us was love. His greatest longing is that we should get to know him, come to love him, enjoy his company. And when we talk to God or listen to him, head to head, heart to heart, this is prayer.'

ANDREW KNOWLES

Being with God

'When you have a great friend you may plan to spend a time with him and may be careful not to miss it. The use of the time is unlikely to be planned, but within the time news may be shared, requests may be made, regrets or gratitude may be spoken, and minds be exchanged, sometimes by talking and listening, and sometimes with little words or gestures ...

To be with God wondering, that is adoration. To be with God gratefully, that is thanksgiving. To be with God ashamed, that is contrition. To be with God with others on the heart, that is intercession. The secret is the quest of God's presence: "Thy face, lord, will I seek." '

MICHAEL RAMSEY

The Lord's Prayer

When Jesus was asked by his followers to teach them to pray, he responded with a model prayer — beautiful, balanced and brief. It has come to be known as the Lord's Prayer.

> *Our Father in heaven,*
> *hallowed be your name,*
> *your kingdom come,*
> *your will be done*
> *on earth as it is in heaven.*
> *Give us today our daily bread.*
> *Forgive us our debts,*
> *as we have forgiven our debtors.*
> *And lead us not into temptation,*
> *but deliver us from the evil one.*

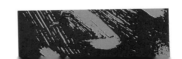

Coming to God

Come near to God and he will come near to you.

FROM THE LETTER TO JAMES

*We must lay before him what is in us,
not what ought to be in us.*

C.S. LEWIS

*God our father, you know my heart, you
understand my thoughts, you are aware how
fragile my faith sometimes is. As I turn now to
prayer, warm my heart, guide my thoughts and
increase my faith. For Jesus Christ's sake. Amen.*

DAVID WINTER

Lord God, I come to you not because I am strong but because I am weak; not because I am full of faith but because I am aware how much I need you; not because I have any right to your blessing but simply because you have invited me to come. Be with me as I pray and help me both to speak and listen. Amen.

DAVID WINTER

Being Quiet Before God

I have stilled and quietened my soul; like a weaned child with its mother, like a weaned child is my soul within me.

FROM PSALM 131

O make my heart so still, so still,
When I am deep in prayer,
That I might hear the whit mist-wreaths
Losing themselves in air!

UTSONOMYA SAN, JAPAN

O God, I cannot begin this day without thee.
I cannot trust myself. Help me, that I may
know that I am not alone.

H.C. ALLEMAN

I find that your will knows no end in me
And when old words die out on the tongue
New melodies break forth from the heart.

RABINDRANATH TAGORE (1861–1941)

Saying Yes to God

Shout for joy to the Lord, all the earth. Worship the Lord with gladness; come before him with joyful songs. Know that the Lord is God. It is he who made us, and we are his . . .

FROM PSALM 100

Lord, you know all things;
you know that I love you.

FROM THE GOSPEL OF JOHN

O Lord, fill us, we beseech thee, with adoring gratitude to thee for all thou art for us, to us, and in us; fill us with love, joy, peace, and all the fruits of the Spirit. Amen.

CHRISTINA ROSSETTI (1830–95)

Set our hearts on fire with love to you, O Christ our God, that in its flame we may love you with all our heart, with all our mind, with all our soul and with all our strength and our neighbours as ourselves, so that, keeping your commandments, we may glorify you, the giver of all good gifts.

EASTERN ORTHODOX CHURCH

Dear Lord, here at the beginning of my life,
I want desparately to know two things:
who I am, and what you would have me to do
with my one life.
I must know, soon.
Could you let me know, Lord?

AUTHOR UNKNOWN

Father in heaven, when the thought of you wakes
in our hearts, let it not wake like a frightened bird
that flies about in dismay, but like a child waking
from its sleep with a heavenly smile.

SÖREN KIERKEGAARD (1813–55)

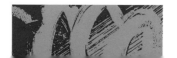

Shone to him the earth and sphere together,
God the Lord has opened a door;
Son of Mary Virgin, hasten thou to help me,
Thou Christ of hope, thou Door of joy,
Golden Sun of hill and mountain,
    All hail! Let there be joy!

GAELIC, 6TH CENTURY

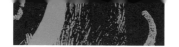

Lord make me an instrument of your
    peace;
Where there is hatred, let me sow love;
Where there is injury, pardon;
Where there is discord, union;
Where there is doubt, faith;
Where there is despair, hope;
Where there is darkness, light;
Where there is sadness, joy.

FRANCIS OF ASSISI

Teach me thy love to know;
That this new light, which now I see,
May both the work and workman show:
Then by a sun-beam I will climb to thee.

GEORGE HERBERT 1593–1633

God of your goodness give me yourself for you
are sufficient for me. I cannot properly ask
anything less, to be worthy of you. If I were to
ask less, I should always be in want. In you alone
do I have all.

JULIAN OF NORWICH, 1342–1443

Daily Life

Everything you do or say, then, should be done in the name of the Lord Jesus, as you give thanks to him through God the Father ... Whatever you do, work at it with all your heart, as though you were working for the Lord, and not for human beings.

FROM PAUL'S LETTER TO THE COLOSSIANS

*Let this day, O Lord, add some knowledge
or good deed to yesterday.*

LANCELOT ANDREWES (1555—1626)

*There is no place
where God is not.
Wherever I go, there God is.
Now and always he upholds
me with his power,
and keeps me safe in
his love.*

AUTHOR UNKNOWN

O Lord, thou knowest how busy I must be this day.
If I forget thee, do not forget me.

SIR JACOB ASTLEY

The day returns and brings us the petty round of
irritating concerns and duties. Help us to play the
man, help us to perform them with laughter and
kind faces. Let cheerfulness abound with industry.
Give us to go blithely on our business all this day,
bring us to our resting beds weary and content
and undishonoured, and grant us in the end the
gift of sleep.

R.L. STEVENSON 1850—94

In the rush and noise of life, as you have intervals,
step home within yourselves and be still. Wait
upon God and feel his good presence; this will carry
you evenly through your day's business.

WILLIAM PENN (1644–1718)

All through this day, O Lord,
by the power of thy quickening Spirit,
let me touch the lives of others for good,
whether through the word I speak,
the prayer I speak,
or the life I live.

AUTHOR UNKNOWN

If indeed it is necessary, O Lord,
to bury the workman that
my work be finished by other hands,
help me never to think of myself as
indispensable.
May I be content to die with my work undone,
knowing that my task
is to work at the fulfilment of thy purposes,
not to work them out.

AUTHOR UNKNOWN

Think often on God, by day, by night, in your business and even in your diversions. He is always near you and with you; leave him not alone.

BROTHER LAWRENCE (1611–91)

Thinking of Others

Love your neighbour as yourself.

JESUS' WORDS IN THE GOSPEL OF LUKE

*O Lord, help me not to despise or oppose
what I do not understand.*

WILLIAM PENN

*Great Spirit, help me never to judge another
until I have walked in his moccasins.*

SIOUX PRAYER

This is my song, O God of all nations,
A song of peace for lands afar, and mine.
This is my hope, the country where my heart is.
This is my hope, my dream, and my shrine.
But other hearts in other lands are beating
With hopes and dreams that are the same as
mine.
My country's skies are bluer than the ocean,
The sunlight beams on clover leafs and pine;
But other lands have sunlight too, and clover,
And other skies are just as blue as mine.
O hear my prayer, thou God of all the nations,
A prayer of peace for other lands and mine.

AUTHOR UNKNOWN

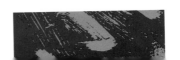

Where the mind is without fear and the head is
*   held high;*
Where knowledge is free;
Where the world has not been broken up into
fragments by narrow domestic walls;
Where words come out from the depth of truth;
Where tireless striving stretches its arm towards
*   perfection;*
Where the clear stream of reason has not lost its
way unto the dreary desert sand of dead habit;
Where the mind is led forward in the
*   ever-widening thought and action —*
Into that heaven of freedom, my Father, let my
*   country awaken*

RABINDRANATH TAGORE

Watch, dear Lord,
with those who wake, or watch, or weep
tonight,
and give your angels charge over those who
sleep.
Tend your sick ones, O Lord Christ,
rest your weary ones.
Bless your dying ones.
Soothe your suffering ones.
Shield your joyous ones.
And all for your love's sake,
Amen.

AUGUSTINE OF HIPPO

Family and Friends

All men will know that you are my disciples
if you love one another.

JESUS' WORDS IN THE GOSPEL OF JOHN

Give us a sense of humour, Lord, and also things to
laugh about. Give us the grace to take a joke
against ourselves, and to see the funny side of the
things we do. Save us from annoyance, bad temper,
resentfulness against our friends. Help us to laugh
even in the face of trouble. Fill our minds with the
love of Jesus; for his name's sake.

A.G. BULLIVANT

Dear Lord,
Help me every day at home.
Help me to show respect
out of love and not just out of duty
and forgive me when I fail.
Forgive me for the times I am selfish and self-
centred,
causing hurt to others in our family.
They make mistakes as well, Lord —
teach me to forgive.
Help me to understand their points of view
and show me how to cope with each problem
as it comes along.
I want to get on with other people
and I know that lesson begins at home.

JANET GREEN

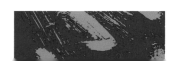

Lord, where would we be without our friends?
They give of themselves unselfishly,
they stand by us in trouble,
in happiness they share our laughter,
they make life more colourful.
Make me a good friend,
ready to help but no to interfere,
loyal but not uncritical,
open rather than exclusive,
dependable at all times.

FROM MORE EVERYDAY PRAYERS

O God, make the door of this house wide enough
to receive all who need human love and
    fellowship,
and a heavenly father's care;
and narrow enough to shut out all envy, pride
    and hate.
Make its threshold smooth enough
to be no stumbling block to children or to straying
    feet,
but rugged enough to turn back the tempter's
    power;
make it a gateway to thine eternal kingdom.

THOMAS KEN (1637–1711),
written at the door of a Christian hospital

Relying on God

What else have I in heaven but you?
Since I have you, what else could I want on earth?

FROM PSALM 73

O Lord,
never suffer us to think
that we can stand by ourselves,
and not need thee.

JOHN DONNE (1573–1631)

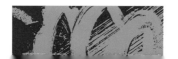

*O Lord Jesus Christ, who art the way, the truth
and the life, we pray thee not to suffer us to stray
from thee, who art the way, nor to distrust thee,
who art the truth, nor to rest on any other than
thee, who art the life. Teach us to believe, what to
do and wherein to take our rest.*

DESIDERIUS ERASMUS (1467–1536)

*Do not be afraid to throw yourself on the Lord!
He will not draw back and let you fall!
Put your worries aside and throw yourself on
    him;
he will welcome you and heal you.*

ST AUGUSTINE (354–430)

Difficult Times

Do not be afraid — I will save you. I have called you by name — you are mine. When you pass through deep waters, I will be with you; your troubles will not overwhelm you.

FROM THE BOOK OF ISAIAH

Be open to the night . . .
Pray with open hand, not with clenched fist.

LORD DUNSANY

O God,
I cannot begin this day without thee.
I cannot trust myself.
Help me,
that I may know that
I am not alone.

H.C. ALLEMAN

It's me, it's me, it's me, O Lord,
Standin' in the need of prayer.
Not my brother, not my sister,
But it's me, O Lord,
Standin' in the need of prayer.

NEGRO SPIRITUAL

I asked the Lord
for a bunch of fresh flowers
but instead he gave me an ugly cactus
with many thorns.
I asked the Lord
for some beautiful butterflies
but instead he gave me
many ugly and dreadful worms.
I was threatened,
I was disappointed,
I mourned.
But after many days,
suddenly,
I saw the cactus bloom
with many beautiful flowers,
and those worms became
beautiful butterflies
flying in the spring wind.
God's way is the best way.

CHUN-MING KAO, WRITTEN FROM PRISON

Like an ant on a stick both ends of which are burning, I go to and fro without knowing what to do and in great despair. Like the inescapable shadow which follows me, the dead weight of sin haunts me. Graciously look upon me. Thy love is my refuge.

PRAYER FROM INDIA

Dear God, be good to me;
The sea is so wide,
And my boat is so small.

BRETON FISHERMAN'S PRAYER

We are weak: out of weakness make us strong.
We are in peril of death: come and heal us.
We believe: help thou our unbelief.
We hope: let us not be disappointed of our hope.
We love: grant us to love much,
to love ever more and more,
to love all,
and most of all to love you.

CHRISTINA ROSSETTI

Father, take all the broken bits of our lives
Our broken promises;
Our broken relationships;
Our differences of opinion,
Our different backgrounds, and shapes, and sizes,
And arrange them together
Fitting them into each other to make something
*   beautiful*
Like an artist makes a stained glass window.
Make a design
Your design
Even when all we can see are the broken bits.

FROM PRAYERS FOR CHILDREN
AND YOUNG PEOPLE

A Fresh Start

Be merciful to me, O God,
because of your constant love.
Because of your great mercy
wipe away my sins!
... Make me a clean heart, O God:
and renew a right spirit within me.

FROM PSALM 51

I have gone astray like a sheep that is lost:
O seek thy servant.

FROM PSALM 119

O Lord, forgive what I have been,
sanctify what I am,
and order what I shall be.

ANONYMOUS

My spirit has become dry because it forgets
to feed on you.

ST JOHN OF THE CROSS (1542–91)

Grant to me, O Lord, true repentance. Help me not just to say that I am sorry, ask forgiveness, and then do the same things all over again; but rather, with your strength to declare war upon everything that is hurtful or displeasing to you.

JOHN EDDISON

Forgive me my sins, O Lord; forgive me the sins of my youth and the sins of mine age, the sins of my soul and the sins of my body, my secret and my whispering sins, my presumptuous and my crying sins, the sins that I have done to please myself and the sins that I have done to please others. Forgive me those sins that I know and those sins which I know not; forgive them, O Lord, forgive them all of thy great goodness.

FROM PRIVATE DEVOTIONS (1560)

Praising God

My heart praises the Lord; my soul is glad
because of God my saviour!

FROM THE GOSPEL OF LUKE

All is silent
In the silent and soundless air,
I fervently bow
To my almighty God.

HSIEH PING-HSIN, CHINA

All you big things bless the Lord
Mount Kilimanjaro and Lake Victoria
The Rift Valley and the Serengeti Plain
Fat baobabs and shady mango trees
All eucalyptus and tamarind trees
Bless the Lord
Praise and extol him for ever and ever.
All you tiny things bless the Lord
Busy black ants and hopping fleas
Wriggling tadpoles and mosquito larvae
Flying locusts and water drops
Pollen dust and tsetse flies
Millet seeds and dried dagga
Bless the Lord
Praise and extol him for ever and ever.

AFRICAN CANTICLE

And now to him who is able to keep us from falling and lift us from the dark valley of despair to the bright mountain of hope, from the midnight of desperation to the daybreak of joy; to him be power and authority, for ever and ever.

MARTIN LUTHER KING

Doing God's Will

Speak, Lord, your servant is listening.

FROM THE FIRST BOOK OF SAMUEL

Lord, take my lips and speak through them;
take my mind and think through it;
take my heart and set it on fire.

W.H.H. AITKEN

We pray ... that you may live a life worthy of the Lord and may please him in every way: bearing fruit in every good work, growing in the knowledge of God, being strengthened with all power according to his glorious might so that you may have great endurance and patience, and joyfully giving thanks to the Father, who has qualified you to share in the inheritance of the saints in the kingdom of light.

FROM THE BOOK OF COLOSSIANS

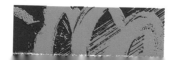

Speak, Lord, for thy servant hears.
Grant us ears to hear,
eyes to see,
wills to obey,
hearts to love;
then declare what thou will,
reveal what thou will,
command what thou will,
demand what thou will — Amen.

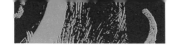

Almighty and everlasting God, grant that our wills be ever meekly subject to your will, and our hearts be ever honestly ready to serve thee. Amen.

ROMAN BREVIARY

What is the work you would have me do, Lord? Please guide me that I may find a job which is worth doing so that I may live full of purpose and joy in serving you, my creator, and helping in this world, whether it be in small ways or with wider responsibilities.

PHYLLIS LOVELOCK

O God our heavenly Father, renew in us the sense of your gracious presence, and let it be a constant impulse within us to peace, trustfulness, and courage on our pilgrimage. Let us hold you fast with a loving and adoring heart, and let our affections be fixed on you, that so the unbroken communion of our hearts with you may accompany us whatever we do, through life and in death. Teach us to pray heartily, to listen for your voice within, and never to stifle its warnings. Behold, we bring our poor hearts as a sacrifice to you: come and fill your sanctuary, and suffer nothing impure to enter there. Let your divine Spirit flow like a river through our whole souls, and lead us in the right way till we pass by a peaceful death into the land of promise. Amen.

GERHARD TERSTEEGEN (1697–1769)

O Lord, you know what is best for us, let this or that be done, as you shall please. Give what you will, and how much you will, and when you will. Deal with us as you think good, and as best pleases you. Set us where you will, and deal with us in all things just as you will. Behold, we are your servants, prepared for all things; for we desire not to live to ourselves, but unto you. And oh, that we could do it worthily and perfectly! Amen.

THOMAS À KEMPIS (1379–1471)

I am only a spark
Make me a fire.
I am only a string
Make me a lyre.
I am only a drop
Make me a fountain.
I am only an ant hill
Make me a mountain.
I am only a feather
Make me a wing.
I am only a rag
Make me a king!

PRAYER FROM MEXICO

Keeping Faith

*Teach me, Lord, what you want me to do,
and I will obey you faithfully; teach me to serve
you with complete devotion.*

FROM PSALM 86

*Almighty God, bestow upon us the meaning of
words, the light of understanding, the nobility of
diction and the faith of the true nature. And grant
that what we believe we may also speak.*

ST HILARY, 315–67

Give us, O Lord, a steadfast heart, which no unworthy affection may drag downwards; give us an unconquered heart, which no tribulation can wear out; give us an upright heart, which no unworthy purpose may tempt aside. Bestow upon us also, O Lord our God, understanding to know you, diligence to seek you, wisdom to find you and a faithfulness that may finally embrace you; through Jesus Christ our Lord.

THOMAS AQUINAS (1225–74)

Blessings

Christ be with me, Christ within me,
Christ behind me, Christ before me,
Christ beside me, Christ to win me,
Christ to comfort and restore me,
Christ beneath me, Christ above me,
Christ in quiet, Christ in danger,
Christ in mouth of friend or stranger.

PATRICK OF IRELAND

May the everlasting Father himself take you
in his own generous clasp,
in his own generous arm.

CELTIC PRAYER

God the Father, bless us;
God the Son, defend us;
God the Spirit, keep us
now and evermore.

FROM LITTLE FOLDED HANDS

The grace of the Lord Jesus Christ
and the love of God
and the fellowship of the Holy Spirit
be with us all.

FROM 2 CORINTHIANS 13

Hear our prayer, O Lord:
bless, protect and sanctify
all those who bow their heads before you.
Through the grace, mercy and love
of your only-begotten Son,
to whom with you and your most holy,
gracious and life-giving Spirit
be blessing now and for ever,
to the ages of ages. Amen.

EASTERN ORTHODOX CHURCH

Acknowledgments

Every attempt has been made to trace copyright holders. If there have been any inadvertent omissions in the acknowledgments we apologize to those concerned.

Concordia Publishing House for material from *Little Folded Hands;*

Janet Green, for 'Dear Lord, Help me every day at home',
from *God's Rules OK*, published by Lion Publishing;

Hodder Headline for material from *Prayers for Children and Young People*,
compiled by Nancy Martin;

National Christian Education Council, for 'Lord, where would we be
without our friends?', from *More Everyday Prayers;*

Walters Books, for John Eddison's 'Grant to me, O Lord, true repentance',
from *Step by Step* by John Eddison.